CAN HUMANS LIVE IN
MARS?

ASTRONOMY BOOK FOR KIDS GRADE 4
CHILDREN'S ASTRONOMY & SPACE BOOKS

First Edition, 2019

Published in the United States by Speedy Publishing LLC, 40 E Main Street, Newark, Delaware 19711 USA.

© 2019 Baby Professor Books, an imprint of Speedy Publishing LLC

Baby Professor Books are available at special discounts when purchased in bulk for industrial and sales-promotional use. For details contact our Special Sales Team at Speedy Publishing LLC, 40 E Main Street, Newark, Delaware 19711 USA. Telephone (888) 248-4521 Fax: (210) 519-4043. www.speedybookstore.com

10 9 8 7 6 * 5 4 3 2 1

Print Edition: 9781541953321
Digital Edition: 9781541956322

See the world in pictures. Build your knowledge in style.
https://www.speedypublishing.com/

TABLE OF CONTENTS

Mars is one of Earth's closest neighbors and a planet that is easily visible without a telescope. The fourth planet in the solar system, Mars is known for its unusual red color. It is its distinctive red hue, in fact, that led ancient cultures to associate the planet with the mythical gods of war. Mars has even been the subject of debate—even in modern times—about where Mars could sustain life.

In this book, we will first examine the characteristics of the fourth planet, Earth's next-door neighbor. We will then look at the information scientists have learned from observations and space missions to Mars to see how this data factors into the question of life on Mars and whether humans can live on the red planet. Let's get started.

Planet Mars

WHERE IS MARS?

Mars is the fourth planet from the Sun. It is located between Earth and Jupiter. Mars is the last of the terrestrial planets or planets that are comprised of rock instead of gasses.

Solar System

On average, Mars is about 141 million miles away from the Sun. Because the orbit of Mars differs than Earth's orbit, the distance between Mars and Earth varies greatly from between 33 million miles to 250 million miles.

Still, Mars is one of Earth's closest neighbors...
close enough for space travel between the two
planets.

Mars is the closest
planet to Earth

A SMALL AND DIVERSE PLANET

Mars is the second smallest of the eight planets

Mars is the second smallest of the eight planets in the Milky Way. Only Mercury, the planet closest to the Sun, is smaller than Mars.

Red planet,
Mars

The red planet is not quite half the size of our own planet. Mars has a diameter of about 2,460 miles. For such a small planet, Mars is geographically diverse.

The tallest mountain on any of the planets is Mars's Olympus Mons, a 17-mile high peak that is more than three times to height of Earth's tallest mountain, Mount Everest.

Mars is also home to the deepest and longest valley in the Milky Way.

An imagf Mars'
deep d long
vey

The Valles Marineris is six miles deep and stretches for about 2,500 rles, about one-fifth of the planet.

The Valles Marineris

WHAT MAKES MARS RED?

Mars loks red in color because its surface is covered with dry, loose rut. The planet has an abundance of iron that turns a dark orge-red color when it oxidizes. Scientists believe that the iron Mars originated more than 4.5 billion years when the Milky W was being formed.

On Earth, the gravity is strong, so iron is pulled into the planet's core. Mars's gravitational pull is much weaker than Earth's, so iron stays on the surface. Iron itself is black in color, but when it is exposed to oxygen, it causes a chemical reaction that produces iron oxide, a red compound.

Mars' gravity is weak so iron stays on its surface.

THE MOVEMENT OF MARS

Mars, like all of the planets, moves in two ways—spinning on its axis and orbiting around the Sun. Mars's axis tilts towards the Sun, just like how Earth's axis does. This creates the seasons because some spots of the planet get more sunlight than others.

Both Mars's and the Earth's axes tilt towards the sun.

How Tilted Are The Planets?

Mercury
0°

Venus
177°

Earth
23°

Mars
25°

Jupiter
3°

Saturn
27°

Uranus
98°

Neptune
28°

Planets not to scale

Mars's seasons, however, are much more extreme than the ones we experience on Earth. One day on Mars is nearly equivalent to one day on Earth, only longer by 39 minutes. Mars's orbit around the Sun is longer than Earth's, too. It is equal to one year and 320 days on Earth.

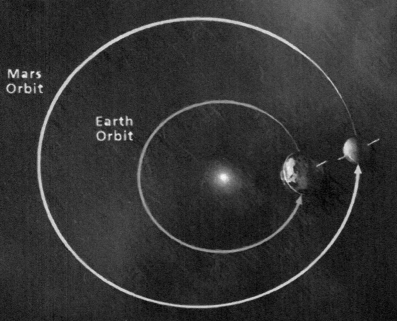

Mars Orbit

Earth Orbit

1 Earth Year = 365 days
1 Mars Year = 687 Earth days or 669 sols (martian days)

Earth and Mars Orbit

Also contributing to Mars's extreme seasons is the fact that this planet's orbit around the Sun is more oval-shaped than circular. Mars has the most elongated orbit of any planet.

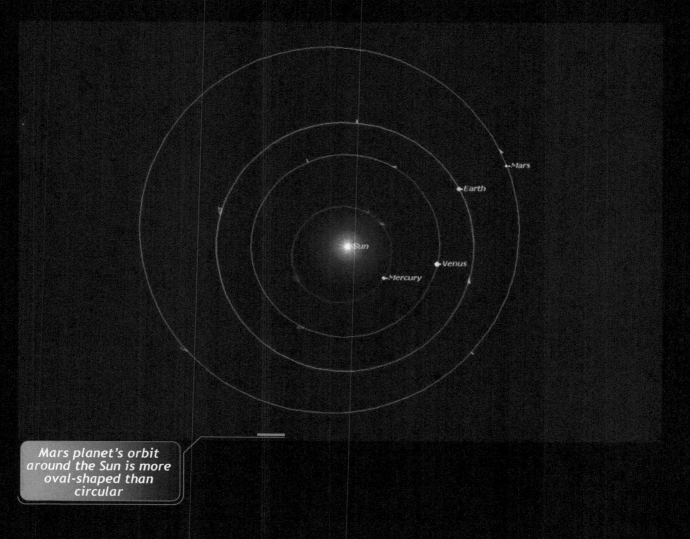

Mars planet's orbit around the Sun is more oval-shaped than circular

THE MOONS OF MARS

There are two small moons that orbit around Mars. Phobos is about 14 miles in diameter, while Deimos is even smaller, only seven and a half miles in diameter. Most scientists believe that both of Mars's moons were once asteroids that got caught in the planet's orbit.

Phobos and Deimos are the two small moons that orbit around Mars

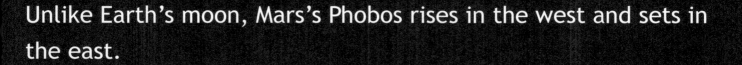

Unlike Earth's moon, Mars's Phobos rises in the west and sets in the east.

Phobos is the innermost and larger of the two natural satellites of Mars

Deimos, on the other hand, rises in the east, but moves slowly. More than two and half days pass between the time that Deimos rises and when it sets in the west.

Mars' smaller moon Deimos

NAMING MARS AND ITS MOONS

Mars is one of the visible planets that has been known to mankind since the beginning of time.

Mars as seen
from earth

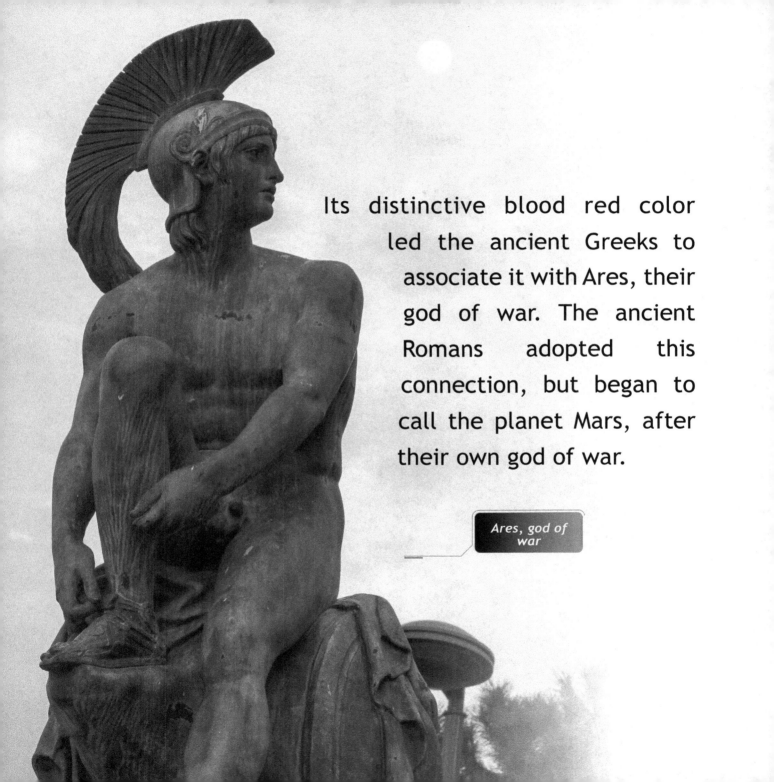

Its distinctive blood red color led the ancient Greeks to associate it with Ares, their god of war. The ancient Romans adopted this connection, but began to call the planet Mars, after their own god of war.

Ares, god of war

When later scientists realized the need for everyone to have the same names for each of the planets, it was decided that they would all share their names with figures in Roman mythology, therefore the red planet officially became known as Mars.

Mars, the god of war in Roman mythology

The standard convention is to name planets after Roman gods, and moons and other celestial bodies after Greek mythology. For that reason, both of Mars's moon, which were discovered in 1877 by Asaph Hall, are named for Greek deities. Phobos, meaning fear, and Deimos, meaning dread, were sidekicks of Ares and joined him in battle.

Asaph Hall

WATER ON
MARS?

Currently, there is no water on the surface of Mars. Instead of oceans, lakes, and rivers, like we see on Earth, Mars is covered with dirt, dust, and rocks.

Mars is covered with dirt, dust, and rocks.

Yet, the planet's surface and rocks show signs of erosion and weathering that could only occur from the movement of water.

Mars's surface and rocks show signs of erosion.

This has led researchers to theorize that Mars did have an abundance of surface water at one time, most likely in the distant past.

Reseachers theorize that Mars had water a long time ago.

Further studies and data collected from space missions to Mars have shown that there is briny water vapor in the atmosphere of Mars, as well as some frozen water in the planet's polar ice caps. Most of the water on the planet evaporated millions of years ago, according to theories put forth by astronomers.

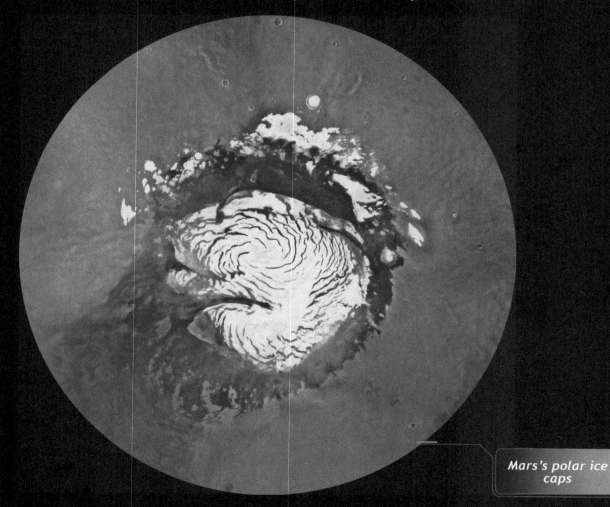

Mars's polar ice caps

WHERE THERE IS WATER, THERE IS LIFE

Most scientists agree that water is a necessary component for life. The presence of water on Mars is an indication that the red planet may have once supported life. In the 1970s, the *Viking* space probes were the first to detect signs of previous organic material on Mars.

Viking **space probes**

Subsequent probes and studies of Mars seem to show that conditions on the planet have changed drastically in the last several million years. It could be that Mars was once more suitable to life.

Conditions on Mars have changed drastically.

NASA released the findings of the *Curiosity* rover in June of 2018 stating that organic material dating back three billion years was found on the surface of Mars. This shows that, at least at one time, the planet had the basic building blocks for life.

NASA's Curiosity
rover

The very next month, NASA announced that they discovered a subglacial lake on Mars, the first confirmed existence of a body of water. Located under the planet's southern ice cap, the discovery of the lake adds credence to the theory that Mars was once suitable for life.

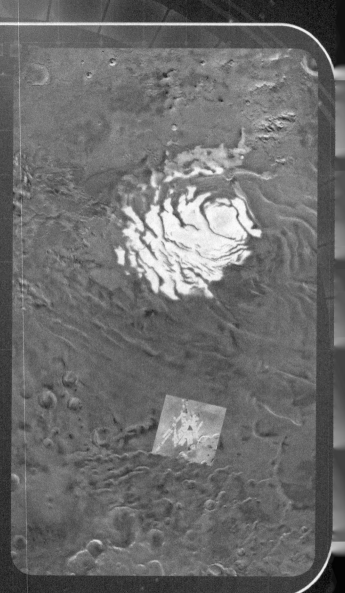

NASA discovered a subglacial lake on Mars

MARTIAN METEORITES FALLING TO EARTH

From time to time, rocks from Mars are expelled from the red planet, usually by an asteroid impact, and land on Earth. These are known as Martian meteorites. So far, geologists have been able to identify more than 200 meteorites as having Martian origins.

An illustration of a Martian meteorites

These unique rocks give scientists a rare opportunity to learn more about the minerals and chemicals found on Mars. One such Martian meteorite, called the Allan Hills 84001, was discovered in December of 1984 in Antarctica.

ALH84001,0

Allan Hills 84001

More than ten years later, scientists studying the rock announced that they saw the fossilized remains of microscopic bacteria in the rock, adding a significant piece of evidence to the theory that Mars once held life.

Scientists found fossilized remains of microscopic bacteria in the Allan Hills 84001

1 μm

Many in the scientific community scoffed at the findings on the Allan Hills 84001 meteorite and those findings are still debated to this day. The Allan Hills 84001 meteorite, and the intense study of this rock, led to the creation of a whole new scientific field—astrobiology.

Allan Hills 84001,
Martian Meteorite,
Smithsonian Museum of
Natural History

OBSERVATIONS OF MARS

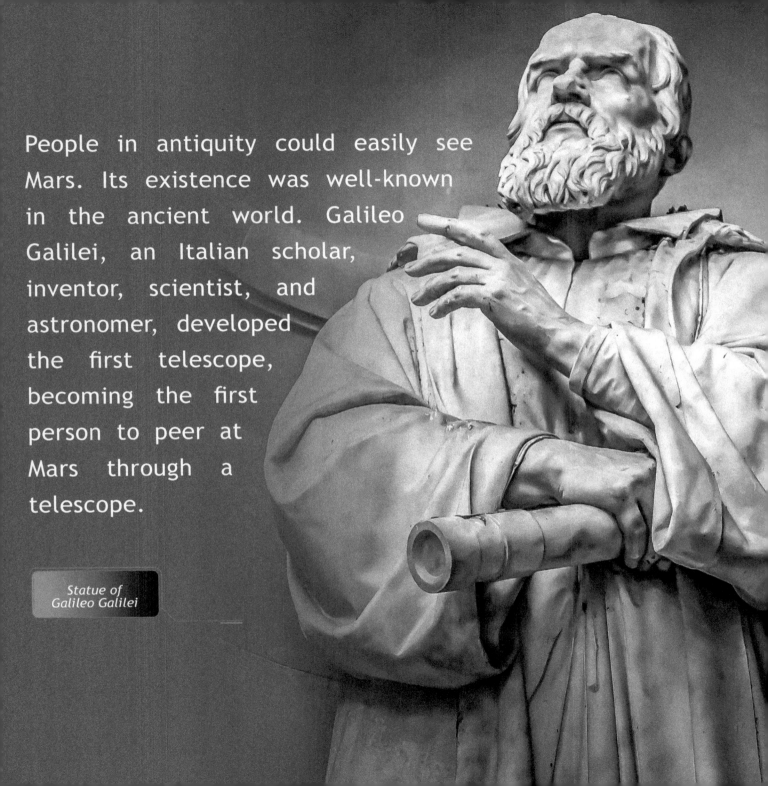

People in antiquity could easily see Mars. Its existence was well-known in the ancient world. Galileo Galilei, an Italian scholar, inventor, scientist, and astronomer, developed the first telescope, becoming the first person to peer at Mars through a telescope.

Statue of Galileo Galilei

Mars at a mere 34,647,420 miles from Earth. Image NASA.

As the power and quality of telescopes improved, astronomers were able to learn more about the red planet.

Beginning in the 1960s, space probes have been sent to Mars to glean even more information from close-up observations. The 1964 unmanned *Mariner 4* and the 1969 *Mariners 6 and 7*, followed by the 1971 *Mariner 9* all added a tremendous volume of information about the planet.

Mariners 6 and 7

Mariner 4 launch

Mariner 9

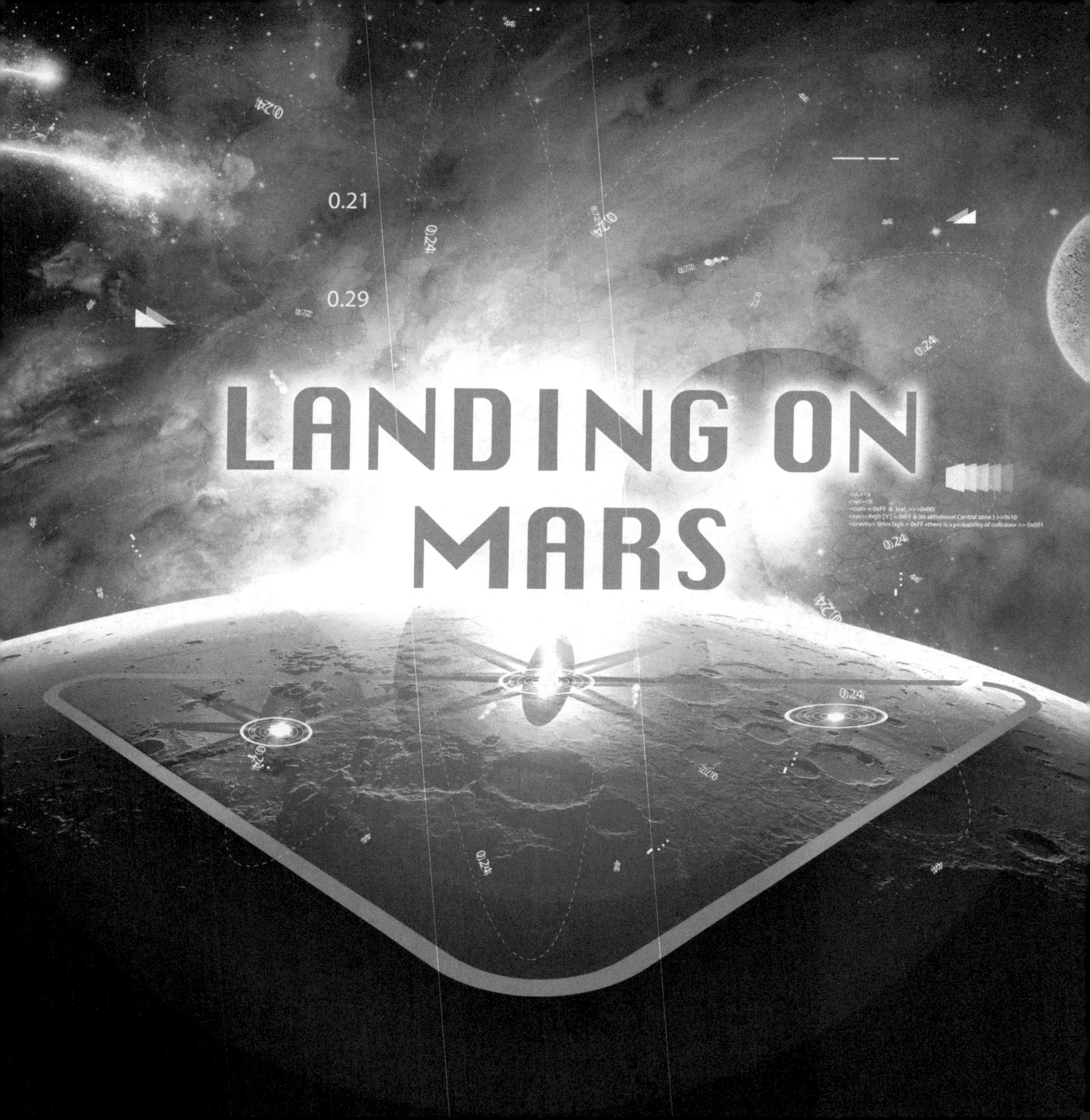
LANDING ON
MARS
0.21
0.29

The first spacecraft to land on the surface of Mars was NASA's *Viking 1* in 1976. The Mars lander was able to take samples of the rocks and dust of the planet but was unable to find water or any signs of life.

Viking 1 on the Martian surface on July 24, 1976

The 1996 *Mars Pathfinder* spacecraft carried with it a rover, called *Sojourner*. It was the task of *Sojourner* to traverse the surface of Mars to analyze the planet's composition.

Mars Pathfinder was launched on a Delta Launch, December 4, 1996

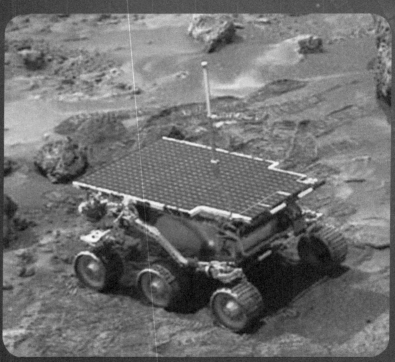

Sojourner

BREAKTHROUGH DISCOVERIES ON MARS

The *Mars Odyssey*, launched by NASA in 2001, was the space probe that discovered frozen water beneath the surface of Mars.

Mars Odyssey

NASA's *Spirit* and *Opportunity*, two rovers launched in 2003, were sent to explore different regions of Mars. Both reported back that they noted evidence that strongly suggests that water once flowed on the surface of Mars.

Spirit Rover

Opportunity Rover

The 2011 *Mars Curiosity* rover discovered complex organic molecules on Mars, and next years' planned mission intends to search for signs of ancient life on the red planet.

Mars Curiosity rover

HUMANS ON MARS

The next logical step in the exploration of Mars is manned missions to the red planet. NASA is currently planning to send astronauts to Mars, but these missions are still a decade away from reality.

An illustration of man on Mars

A voyage to Mars, with today's rocket technology, would still take several months to complete, meaning that the astronauts would have to endure several months of zero gravity before they even reached Mars.

A 3D illustration of a spacecraft travelling towards Mars.

The lack of gravity has a profound effect on the human body, so the astronauts may not even be able to complete their assigned tasks once they get to Mars. NASA is currently working with other space agencies to resolve these challenges in preparation for future manned missions to Mars.

The surface gravity on Mars is less than the surface gravity on Earth

SUMMARY

While humans cannot live on Mars, that doesn't mean that the red planet didn't once harbor life or that humans won't visit there one day. It could be that microscopic life did once exist on Mars, but that conditions on the planet changed so that it became unsuitable for life.

A 3d illustration of Mars's surface

There is evidence that there used to be flowing water on the surface of the planet and that water can still be found there deep underground. The building blocks of life were once present on Mars. Perhaps future manned space missions to the red planet will show us if life could, once again, thrive there.

Now that you understand more about Mars, the red planet, you should consider reading up on some of the other planets in our solar system. Each one is unique. Learning about them helps us to understand more about our own planet, Earth.

Visit

www.BabyProfessorBooks.com

to download Free Baby Professor
eBooks and view our catalog of new
and exciting Children's Books

CPSIA information can be obtained
at www.ICGtesting.com
Printed in the USA
JSHW031935290322
24117JS00002BC/112